SONNET 116

*L*et me not to the marriage of true minds

Admit impediments. Love is not love

Which alters when it alteration finds,

Or bends with the remover to remove.

O no! it is an ever-fixèd mark

That looks on tempests and is never shaken;

It is the star to every wandering bark,

Whose worth's unknown, although his height be taken.

Love's not Time's fool, though rosy lips and cheeks

Within his bending sickle's compass come:

Love alters not with his brief hours and weeks,

But bears it out even to the edge of doom.

    If this be error and upon me proved,

    I never writ, nor no man ever loved.

WILLIAM SHAKESPEARE | JENNIFER FANDEL

PHOTOGRAPHS BY | MARCEL IMSAND

You are holding in your hands a biography of the greatest poet in English—and perhaps in any language. Homer, Dante, Tolstoy, Dickens, and other writers are justly famous, but their literary reputations do not compare with William Shakespeare's (1564–1616). He is best known as a poetic dramatist for his tragedies, comedies, and historical plays. Even nearly 400 years after his death, his tragedies in particular—among them *Hamlet*, *King Lear*, *Romeo and Juliet*, *Othello*, and *Macbeth*—are the touchstones of world literature.

Shakespeare did not enjoy a royal upbringing. Although by English law, students were taught Latin and the classics, his early life in the rural town of Stratford-upon-Avon did not foretell literary success. He married at 18 and fathered 3 children with Anne Hathaway, but soon he was off to seek his fortune in London.

After a decade-long gap in Shakespeare's exact whereabouts—"the lost years"—he reappeared in 1592 on the London theater scene. He went on to write at least 37 plays, 154 sonnets, and 2 long narrative poems, works that have been translated into every major language.

Shakespeare's renowned plays demonstrate "a sea of troubles," the fatal flaws to which humans are heirs: deceit, intrigue, jealousy, self-doubt, and hasty errors in judgment. Which of Shakespeare's personal experiences went into his writing? History cannot tell us. What is clear is that his poetry was superior to the verse of any of his contemporaries—a reflection of his mastery of language and the intensity of his vision.

Shakespeare's first 126 sonnets are written to a "fair youth" or "rival poet," the following 28 to a "dark lady." The characters' identities remain unknown. A few of the sonnets are outright declarations of devotion, but the overarching theme of these 14-line poems is the permanence of change: youth and beauty pass, love grows and fades, death is inevitable. Yet nothing in literature seems more certain than the permanence of William Shakespeare's genius.

– J. Patrick Lewis, United States Children's Poet Laureate (2011-13)

INTRODUCTION

"He was not of an age, but for all time."

– British poet Ben Jonson, on Shakespeare

Nearly 400 years after his death, William Shakespeare is a name recognized in every language, carrying with it connotations of tragedy, romance, and love. While Shakespeare is most widely celebrated through theatrical performances of his plays, people all over the world have quietly continued to read his most famous poems, the sonnets, savoring each word and the emotions that rage, sing, and linger on the page.

Shakespeare left behind little evidence of his life besides the immense amount of work he produced. In total, he authored 37 surviving plays, 2 narrative poems, and 154 sonnets—all within a time span of approximately 30 years. Deemed the "English National Poet" and "The Bard of Avon," Shakespeare continues to be honored for his creative genius and his ingenuity with language. But it is for a much grander accomplishment that Shakespeare has been placed on a pedestal in the world of literature, for no one since has so passionately and so earnestly connected to the human experience.

William Shakespeare at work

SONNET 18

$\mathcal{S}$hall I compare thee to a summer's day?

Thou art more lovely and more temperate:

Rough winds do shake the darling buds of May,

And summer's lease hath all too short a date;

Sometime too hot the eye of heaven shines,

And often is his gold complexion dimm'd,

And every fair from fair sometime declines,

By chance or nature's changing course untrimm'd;

But thy eternal summer shall not fade,

Nor lose possession of that fair thou ow'st,

Nor shall Death brag thou wand'rest in his shade,

When in eternal lines to time thou grow'st;

    So long as men can breathe or eyes can see,

    So long lives this, and this gives life to thee.

William Shakespeare was born on April 23, 1564, in the small agricultural market town of Stratford-upon-Avon in England. He was the third child born to Mary Arden and John Shakespeare, but he was the first of their children to survive past infancy.

The Stratford of William Shakespeare's youth was a peaceful town surrounded by farms, woods, fields, and the flow of the river Avon. Despite its rural setting, it was a town nestled in the crossroads of travel and commerce. William's father ran a successful business as a glover and leather-worker in Stratford, and he also dealt in moneylending and wool. Because of his skill as a businessman, John Shakespeare was elected to the post of high bailiff, or mayor. His position in the town likely provided some advantages for William and the rest of the family.

During the latter half of the 16th century, theater was becoming a popular form of entertainment in England. Professional theater companies from London began touring the country, usually stopping twice a year in market towns such as Stratford.

Shakespeare's birthplace

Often the high bailiff welcomed the players and screened their performances to make sure they were fit for the public. Many scholars believe that William's father brought his son along to view these private performances. William most likely attended his first professional theater performance at the age of 11. But, before that time, he may have seen amateur performances of mummer's plays and mystery plays, both of which involved stories from the Bible. Morality plays were also popular, as were festive events such as pageants and masques. All these performances were sure to have had an impact on the early development of William's dramatic and poetic interests.

A morality play performance, late 1500s

To-morrow, and to-morrow, and to-morrow,

Creeps in this petty pace from day to day,

To the last syllable of recorded time;

And all our yesterdays have lighted fools

The way to dusty death. Out, out, brief candle!

Life's but a walking shadow, a poor player,

That struts and frets his hour upon the stage,

And then is heard no more. It is a tale

Told by an idiot, full of sound and fury,

Signifying nothing.

From *Macbeth*, act 5, scene 5

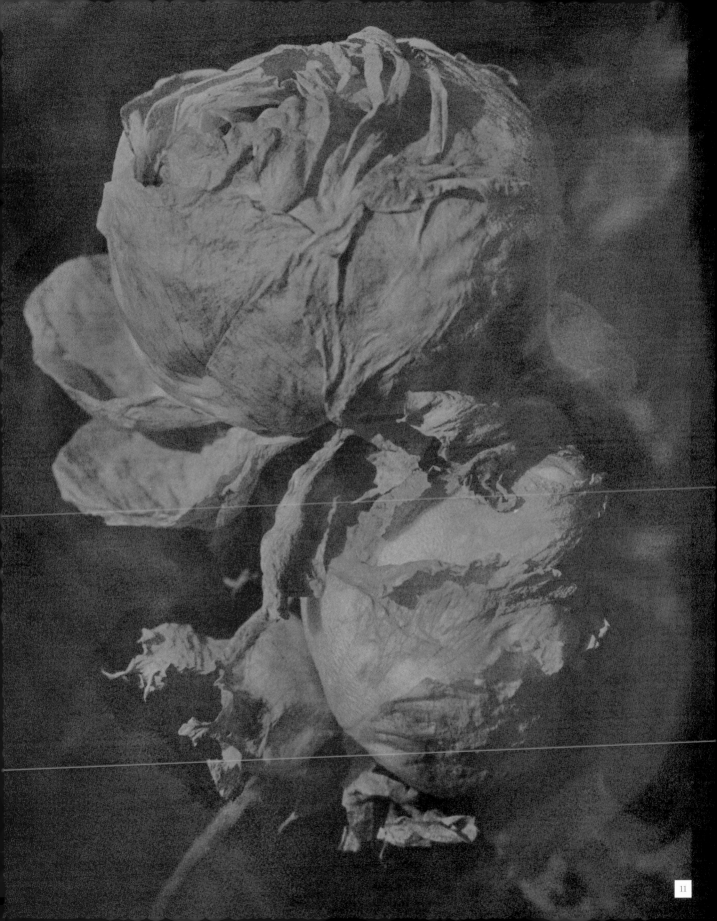

SCHOOL DAYS

At the age of five, William began attending school six days a week at the New King's School in Stratford with other boys in the community. The long school day began around seven in the morning and ended around five at night; students were permitted a few hours for lunch before going back to finish their lessons: Latin grammar, poems, and dramas; Roman comedies; some Greek language and literature; and study of the Bible.

At the age of 12 or 13, William was removed from school to serve as an apprentice to his father. John Shakespeare's business dealings were beginning to suffer, and he now had five more children to feed. As the eldest child in the family, William likely shouldered some of the burden to help the family make ends meet. However, it is thought that William did not spend all his teenage years working. He found time for play and romance in the fresh country air of Stratford, courting the woman who was soon to become his wife.

Shakespeare as a young man

SONNET 29

When in disgrace with Fortune and men's eyes
I all alone beweep my outcast state,
And trouble deaf heaven with my bootless cries,
And look upon myself and curse my fate,
Wishing me like to one more rich in hope,
Featur'd like him, like him with friends possess'd,
Desiring this man's art, and that man's scope,
With what I most enjoy contented least;
Yet in these thoughts myself almost despising,
Haply I think on thee, and then my state
(Like to the lark at break of day arising
From sullen earth) sings hymns at heaven's gate,
  For thy sweet love rememb'red such wealth brings,
  That then I scorn to change my state with kings.

LOST YEARS

In 1582, at the age of 18, William married Anne Hathaway. The marriage was a hurried affair, taking place in secret rather than in a common public ceremony. Because Anne had conceived William's child out of wedlock, their private ceremony was probably intended to spare their families from shame. Six months after their marriage, in May 1583, the couple's first child, Susanna, was born. Two years later, William and Anne welcomed twins, a girl and a boy, into their family. The girl, Judith, was a healthy child, but the boy, Hamnet, did not live through his later childhood years.

There is little record of William's life from age 18 to 28 other than the documents that mark major events such as his marriage and his children's births. It is not known what William did to support his new family at the time, but within two years of the twins' birth, William was no longer living in Stratford; he

English women's fashions of the late 16th century

was journeying toward London the only way a man of his limited means could: he walked. He would see his wife and children little in the next 11 years, most likely visiting only once a year.

London was a booming city attractive to entrepreneurs, artists, and excitement-seekers. It is probable that William's journey took him directly to the big city, for that is where he settled. Some experts have surmised that he worked as a country schoolmaster along the way, that he worked for lawyers, or that some sort of trouble cast him out of the quiet, country life of Stratford. No one knows for sure. But no matter what William did during the lost years, he was found in 1592 at the age of 28. Documents from that time speak of him as a prosperous playwright well known to others in the field.

London, the capital of England

SONNET 50

How heavy do I journey on the way,
When what I seek (my weary travel's end)
Doth teach that ease and that repose to say,
"Thus far the miles are measur'd from thy friend."
The beast that bears me, tired with my woe,
Plods dully on, to bear that weight in me,
As if by some instinct the wretch did know
His rider lov'd not speed, being made from thee.
The bloody spur cannot provoke him on,
That sometimes anger thrusts into his hide,
Which heavily he answers with a groan,
More sharp to me than spurring to his side,
    For that same groan doth put this in my mind:
    My grief lies onward and my joy behind.

LONDON

When Queen Elizabeth took the throne in 1558, an exhilarating era began in England. Interest in the arts, politics, and world affairs blossomed throughout the country. England rose as an international power, and this newfound status swelled citizens with pride in their nation and in the English language. Before this time, England had often looked to continental Europe, especially France and Italy, in admiration of their arts, literature, and theater. Little English poetry had been published, and no English plays were known to have been written before the time of Shakespeare's birth. But with the coronation of Elizabeth I came a transformation in the culture and art of the nation. England began to recognize the talents of its own citizens. Education was encouraged, increasing literacy, and people grew more curious to see and enjoy the world around them. An interest in English poetry developed among literary audiences, and numerous theaters were constructed around London.

Because of the opportunities present during Shakespeare's lifetime, London attracted citizens from throughout the country, and the city soon doubled in size. By the end of Queen Elizabeth's reign, in 1603, London had grown to include 200,000 inhabitants. Among that bustling crowd, William Shakespeare had firmly taken his place. It was within this artistic wonderland that Shakespeare's writing career developed and thrived.

Such wind as scatters young men through the world

To seek their fortunes farther than at home,

Where small experience grows. But in a few,

Signior Hortensio, thus it stands with me:

Antonio, my father, is deceas'd,

And I have thrust myself into this maze,

Happily to wive and thrive as best I may.

Crowns in my purse I have, and goods at home,

And so am come abroad to see the world.

From *The Taming of the Shrew*, act 1, scene 2

THEATER

William Shakespeare's days in London abounded with theater life. Initially, he took to the stage as an actor for The Lord Chamberlain's Men, but he soon received praise not for his acting but for the magnificent plays he was writing. His ability to capture the interests and imaginations of playgoers of that time testifies to his talent, as many theatergoers paid more attention to the rowdy scenes occurring within the audience than they did to the play itself.

The theater was divided into higher-priced balcony seats and the cheap floor space, where the groundlings stood. Since pleasure was the purpose of attending, many of the groundlings spent their time during the performance drinking and laughing, sometimes heckling the actors. But Shakespeare's plays worked an unusual magic on audiences. His works possessed a daring mixture of violence and romance, and Shakespeare's words brought his audiences straight into the heart of each and every character.

By 1592, Shakespeare was well established as an actor and playwright in London. Even though the 28-year-old was in high demand as a playwright, he made little money for the writing he did, and he made even less money for his acting. Ironically, it was his business sense that helped him prosper. Shakespeare became part owner of London's Globe Theater, which became the home of The Lord Chamberlain's Men, the theater company he co-owned with actors Richard Burbage, Henry Condell, and John Heminge. Shakespeare stayed with The Lord Chamberlain's Men, later called The King's Men, until the end of his theatrical career. His allegiances to his partners, and theirs to him, proved unshakable in the years to come.

London's Globe Theater, c. 1600

Speak the speech, I pray you, as I pronounc'd it to
you, trippingly on the tongue: but if you mouth it,
as many of your players do, I had as lief the
town-crier spoke my lines. Nor do not saw the air
too much with your hand, thus, but use all gently;
for in the very torrent, tempest, and, as I may say,
whirlwind of your passion, you must acquire and beget
a temperance that may give it smoothness. O, it
offends me to the soul to hear a robustious
periwig-pated fellow tear a passion to tatters, to
very rags, to split the ears of the groundlings, who
for the most part are capable of nothing but
inexplicable dumb-shows and noise....

Be not too tame neither, but let your own discretion
be your tutor. Suit the action to the word, the
word to the action, with this special observance,
that you o'erstep not the modesty of nature: for any
thing so o'erdone is from the purpose of playing,
whose end, both at the first and now, was and is,
to hold as 'twere, the mirror up to nature: to show
virtue her own feature, scorn her own image, and
the very age and body of the time his form and pressure.
Now this overdone, or come tardy off, though it make
the unskillful laugh, cannot but make the judicious grieve;
the censure of which one must in your allowance o'erweigh
a whole theatre of others.

From *Hamlet*, act 3, scene 2

Der Doctor Schna- -bel von Rom.

PLAGUE

From 1592 through 1594, all theaters in London were closed by order of the queen. People were dying in large numbers as the bubonic plague, also called the Black Death, ravaged London. At its peak, 1,000 people died each week. In total, the plague claimed nearly 11,000 lives within a 7-mile (11 km) radius of London. Scholars have presumed that during this time Shakespeare fled to Stratford, where the plague had not spread.

With the playhouses closed and no immediate income available, Shakespeare had to find other means of making a living. Even though he continued to write plays, poetry may have been his way out of the financial difficulties and emotional darkness of the plague. Scholars believe that Shakespeare wrote his 2 narrative poems, and perhaps some of

his 154 sonnets, at this time. "Venus and Adonis," dedicated to the Earl of Southampton, was the first of Shakespeare's poems to gain attention. Published in 1593, "Venus and Adonis" revealed Shakespeare's talent for combining pleasure and the intellect, thrilling the court society and a cultivated London audience.

The popularity of "Venus and Adonis" led to more printings of the poem and a growing audience for Shakespeare's poetic work as well as the patronage of the Earl of Southampton. It is believed that the Earl, after reading the romantic and slightly scandalous poem, provided Shakespeare with a sizable sum of money to continue with his poetry. This money eased Shakespeare's worries during the plague years and fueled his poetic genius.

A physician in protective plague clothing

SONNET 65

Since brass, nor stone, nor earth, nor boundless sea,
But sad mortality o'ersways their power,
How with this rage shall beauty hold a plea,
Whose action is no stronger than a flower?
O how shall summer's honey breath hold out
Against the wrackful siege of batt'ring days,
When rocks impregnable are not so stout,

Nor gates of steel so strong, but Time decays?
O fearful meditation! where, alack,
Shall Time's best jewel from Time's chest lie hid?
Or what strong hand can hold his swift foot back?
Or who his spoil of beauty can forbid?
　　O none, unless this miracle have might,
　　That in black ink my love may still shine bright.

Shakespeare popularized the poetic form that came to be known as the Elizabethan or Shakespearean sonnet. Meaning "little song," the sonnet is a condensed, 14-line, rhyming poem. Sonnet sequences, which are groups of sonnets that tell a story or are unified by a theme, were in vogue during the early part of Shakespeare's writing career; he was likely influenced by this trend, as many of his sonnets seem to work together thematically. Scholars are not sure, however, of the true order of Shakespeare's sonnets, since he was not involved in and had not authorized the publication of those poems.

Controversy has marked Shakespeare's sonnets ever since their publication. Scholars have pondered the subjects of them for years, referring to the characters as the young man (or youth), the dark lady, and the rival poet. Even the dates of composition are subject to debate. Some experts cite the period 1593 through 1599 as the years when Shakespeare may have written the majority of his sonnets. The early date follows Shakespeare's success with "Venus and Adonis," and the later date coincides with some of the comments made by writers and critics about Shakespeare's "sugared sonnets" circulating among his friends.

Despite all the speculation, the sonnets continue to be popular with readers because of their universal truths about love and legacy. No matter whom Shakespeare had in mind when he wrote his poems, readers appreciate his sonnets for their intimacy and honesty as well as the stunning language and music that rise from the page. In 1598, the critic Francis Meres described Shakespeare as one of "the most passionate among us to bewail and bemoan the perplexities of love." When reading the sonnets, that is all most readers feel they need to know.

Shakespeare depicted at his peak

SHAKE-SPEARES

SONNETS.

Neuer before Imprinted.

_____

_____

AT LONDON
By *G. Eld* for *T. T.* and are
to be folde by *Iohn Wright*, dwelling
at Chrift Church gate.
1 6 0 9.

SONNET 130

My mistress' eyes are nothing like the sun;
Coral is far more red than her lips' red;
If snow be white, why then her breasts are dun;
If hairs be wires, black wires grow on her head.
I have seen roses damask'd, red and white,
But no such roses see I in her cheeks,
And in some perfumes is there more delight
Than in the breath that from my mistress reeks.
I love to hear her speak, yet well I know
That music hath a far more pleasing sound;
I grant I never saw a goddess go,
My mistress when she walks treads on the ground.
  And yet, by heaven, I think my love as rare
  As any she belied with false compare.

A
PLEASANT
Conceited Comedie
CALLED,
Loues labors loſt.

As it vvas preſented before her Highnes
this laſt Chriſtmas.

Newly corrected and augmented
By W. Shakeſpere

Imprinted at London by *W.W.*
for *Cutbert Burby*.
1598.

P U B L I S H I N G

Because the majority of people could not read before Shakespeare's time, there was little demand for more than a few manuscripts that could be circulated among scholars. But education of the masses changed that, just as the increased use of the printing press made the production of more manuscripts much easier. Despite the recognition that printing often brought writers, Shakespeare adhered to his own ideas about publishing.

Even though Shakespeare was highly regarded for his playwriting skills, he never saw himself as any more than a craftsman for the stage. He didn't believe, as was common at the time, that plays were literature. Shakespeare's only printed play during his lifetime was *Love's Labor's Lost*, in 1598. After his death, his friends from The King's Men, John Heminge and Henry Condell, decided that his plays must be published to preserve his word and genius. The First Folio, the first collection of Shakespeare's plays, was published seven years after his death.

Shakespeare's first published play

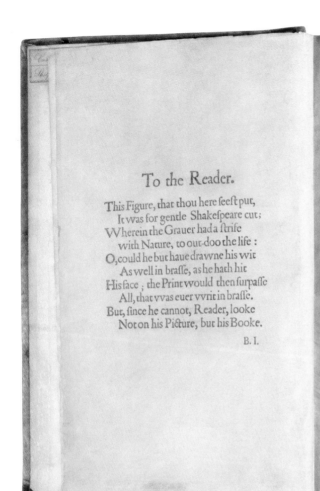

Shakespeare, however, felt a bit differently about his poetry. His narrative poem "Venus and Adonis" marked the debut of Shakespeare's published poetry in 1593. It was an enormous success, establishing Shakespeare as a "poet of love." Many people purchased "Venus and Adonis," which went through 16 printings before 1640. No other work by any other writer achieved so many printings during this period. His second published poem was "The Rape of Lucrece," another narrative poem. Published in 1594, it was not as successful as "Venus and Adonis," but it was still reprinted eight times before 1640.

Shakespeare's sonnets, on the contrary, were not published with his permission. No one knows why Shakespeare did not pursue their publication—whether he felt they were too personal remains a mystery. Since Shakespeare circulated his sonnets among friends in manuscript form, it is presumed that through this link the publisher Thomas Thorpe obtained Shakespeare's poems, which he published in 1609.

The First Folio, 1623

SONNET 55

Not marble nor the gilded monuments
Of princes shall outlive this pow'rful rhyme,
But you shall shine more bright in these contents
Than unswept stone, besmear'd with sluttish time.
When wasteful war shall statues overturn,
And broils root out the work of masonry,
Nor Mars his sword nor war's quick fire shall burn
The living record of your memory.
'Gainst death and all-oblivious enmity
Shall you pace forth; your praise shall still find room,
Even in the eyes of all posterity
That wear this world out to the ending doom.
 So till the judgment that yourself arise,
 You live in this, and dwell in lovers' eyes.

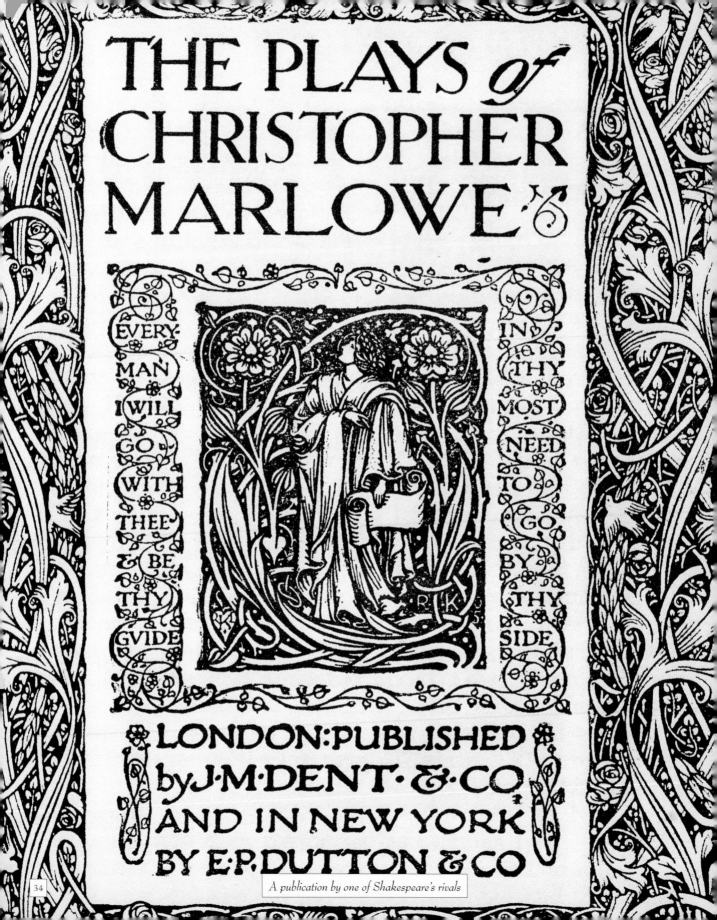

THE PLAYS of CHRISTOPHER MARLOWE

EVERY MAN I WILL GO WITH THEE & BE THY GVIDE

IN THY MOST NEED TO GO BY THY SIDE

LONDON: PUBLISHED by J·M·DENT·&·CO. AND IN NEW YORK BY E·P·DUTTON & CO

A publication by one of Shakespeare's rivals

CONTEMPORARIES

Shakespeare's acquaintances, friends, enemies, and competitors all left their marks on his life and his work. One such acquaintance, Christopher Marlowe, was a talented writer admired for his innovative merging of literary and popular writing, attracting a wide public audience. Because he had attended a university, his work was also embraced by literary critics and scholars. Shakespeare respected Marlowe's work but possessed none of his advantages. Nonetheless, Marlowe often competed with Shakespeare and may have challenged him for the Earl of Southampton's financial support. In a twist of fate, however, Marlowe was killed in 1593 during a tavern brawl with another writer, thus ending Shakespeare's competition with him.

A typical 17th-century London tavern

English dramatist and poet Ben Jonson

Ben Jonson was another writer who influenced Shakespeare. Eight years younger, Jonson was also brought up in a business family, becoming a brick-layer's apprentice, since he had neither the wealth nor the ties to attend college. He drifted to the theater and began acting, although it has been said that he lacked talent. But then he pursued writing, and his plays were quickly hailed for their insight and intellect. Even though competition existed between the two men, Jonson's poem in memorial to Shakespeare reveals that a deep respect also existed.

Less competition and more camaraderie existed within The King's Men, the actors perhaps serving as Shakespeare's second family when he was so often away from his own. Shakespeare's partners, the actors John Heminge, Henry Condell, and Richard Burbage, all thought well of Shakespeare and referred to him as "Gentle Will Shakespeare." Their love and admiration for their old friend is evident in the dedication they wrote for the First Folio:

We have but collected them [the plays], and done an office to the dead, to procure his orphans, guardians; without ambition either of self-profit, or fame; only to keep the memory of so worthy a friend, and fellow alive, as was our Shakespeare....

SONNET 30

When to the sessions of sweet silent thought
I summon up remembrance of things past,
I sigh the lack of many a thing I sought,
And with old woes new wail my dear time's waste;
Then can I drown an eye (unus'd to flow)
For precious friends hid in death's dateless night,
And weep afresh love's long since cancell'd woe,
And moan th' expense of many a vanish'd sight;
Then can I grieve at grievances foregone,
And heavily from woe to woe tell o'er
The sad account of fore-bemoaned moan,
Which I new pay as if not paid before:
　　But if the while I think on thee, dear friend,
　　All losses are restor'd, and sorrows end.

FINALE

Between the years of 1610 and 1611, at the age of 46, Shakespeare moved back to Stratford as a wealthy gentleman. He continued to write plays and hold his connections to the Globe Theater, but in 1613, the Globe burned down, marking Shakespeare's retirement from the theater. Shakespeare owned property that his father had left him in his will, and he also invested much of his own money in Stratford property. He purchased New Place in 1597, which had become his family's official residence and his new home upon retirement. The second-largest house in Stratford, New Place sat on an acre (0.4 ha) of land and had two barns and two orchards.

The town eagerly welcomed a gentleman back into its fold, and even though Shakespeare seldom involved himself in Stratford affairs, he liked the townspeople immensely. When he desired the excitement of intellectual debate and artistic discussions, he invited fellow theater and writing friends to his Stratford home, entertaining them for hours on end. It was one of these nights of revelry that may, in fact, have caused his death.

Shakespeare entertained Ben Jonson and the poet Michael Brayton one night in April 1616. They had a pleasurable time together, drinking much wine, eating pickled herrings, and likely boasting and laughing about their lives. Soon after this night, Shakespeare fell ill. He died on his birthday, April 23, at the age of 52, and was buried 2 days later inside the chancel of the Holy Trinity Church in Stratford. No one knows if these darkly humorous lines were written by Shakespeare, but the following epitaph appears on his tomb:

Good frend for Jesus sake forbeare,
To digg the dust encloased heere.
Blese be ye man [that] spares thes stones,
And curst be he [that] moves my bones.

Shakespeare's home in Stratford-upon-Avon

William Shakespeare, 1564–1616

All the world's a stage,
And all the men and women merely players;
They have their exits and their entrances,
And one man in his time plays many parts,
His acts being seven ages. At first, the infant,
Mewling and puking in the nurse's arms.
Then the whining schoolboy, with his satchel
And shining morning face, creeping like snail
Unwillingly to school. And then the lover,
Sighing like a furnace, with a woeful ballad
Made to his mistress' eyebrow. Then a soldier,
Full of strange oaths, and bearded like the pard,
Jealous in honor, sudden and quick in quarrel,
Seeking the bubble reputation
Even in the cannon's mouth. And then the justice,
In fair round belly with good capon lined,
With eyes severe and beard of formal cut,
Full of wise saws and modern instances;
And so he plays his part. The sixth age shifts
Into the lean and slippered pantaloon,
With spectacles on nose and pouch on side,
His youthful hose, well saved, a world too wide
For his shrunk shank, and his big manly voice,
Turning again toward childish treble, pipes
And whistles in his sound. Last scene of all,
That ends this strange eventful history,
Is second childishness and mere oblivion,
Sans teeth, sans eyes, sans taste, sans everything.

From *As You Like It*, act 2, scene 7

IMMORTALITY

During Shakespeare's lifetime, many scholars and writers disregarded his work because he was not a university-schooled man. Following his death, critics began to change their minds, recognizing what is referred to as Shakespeare's "universal genius." Shakespeare did not possess the advantages of the royal or elite, but his hard-earned life as a writer seemed to cultivate a greater sensitivity and awareness of the world around him. Many consider Shakespeare a "poet of the people" because he drew from the life that he observed and the language that he heard among the common people from which he came. His poems and plays reflect a keen interest in all subjects, containing references to the world he knew through experience and the world he understood through books. Shakespeare's singular approach is reflected in the literary and popular appeal of his work, something that was seldom seen at the time.

Since Shakespeare's death, people from around the world have flocked to England, ardent in their quests to see the places once touched by the poet. They have made pilgrimages to his grave in Stratford and have stood before his statue in London's Westminster Abbey, feeling Shakespeare's presence alive in the air. But looking upon the monuments to his greatness is of little consequence. For as solid as these testaments to his life and work stand, it is in the hearts and minds of his readers that Shakespeare's words will continue to endure.

SONNET 73

That time of year thou mayst in me behold
When yellow leaves, or none, or few, do hang
Upon those boughs which shake against the cold,
Bare ruin'd choirs, where late the sweet birds sang.
In me thou see'st the twilight of such day
As after sunset fadeth in the west,
Which by and by black night doth take away,

Death's second self, that seals up all in rest.
In me thou see'st the glowing of such fire
That on the ashes of his youth doth lie,
As the death-bed whereon it must expire,
Consum'd with that which it was nourish'd by.
    This thou perceiv'st, which makes thy love more strong,
    To love that well, which thou must leave ere long.

ACKNOWLEDGMENTS

PHOTO CREDITS

Corbis (Archivio Iconografico, S.A., Nathan Benn, Bettmann, Stefano Bianchetti, Michael Nicholson), Hulton Archive, North Wind Picture Archives, Timepix (Thomas D. McAvoy)

PLAY EXCERPTS & POETRY CREDITS

The Riverside Shakespeare, edited by G. Blakemore Evans. Copyright © 1974 by Houghton Mifflin Company. Used with permission.

SELECTED WORKS BY WILLIAM SHAKESPEARE

COMEDIES
As You Like It
Love's Labor's Lost
Measure for Measure
A Midsummer Night's Dream
Much Ado About Nothing
The Taming of the Shrew
Twelfth Night

POEMS
154 Sonnets
"The Rape of Lucrece"
"Venus and Adonis"

HISTORIES
Henry IV, Part I
Henry V
King John
Richard II
Richard III

TRAGEDIES
Hamlet
King Lear
Macbeth
Othello
Romeo and Juliet

INDEX

Published by Creative Paperbacks
P.O. Box 227, Mankato, Minnesota 56002
Creative Paperbacks is an imprint of The Creative Company
www.thecreativecompany.us
Design by Stephanie Blumenthal
Production by The Design Lab
Artwork by Marcel Imsand
Art direction by Rita Marshall
Printed in the United States of America

Library of Congress Cataloging-in-Publication Data
Fandel, Jennifer.
William Shakespeare / by Jennifer Fandel.
p. cm. — (Voices in Poetry)
Includes index.
Summary: An exploration of the life and work of 16th-century
English writer William Shakespeare, whose poetry is known best for
its sonnet form as well as its transcendent descriptions of love.
ISBN 978-1-60818-328-9 (hardcover)
ISBN 978-1-62832-056-5 (pbk)
1. Shakespeare, William, 1564–1616—Juvenile literature. 2. Dramatists,
English—Early modern, 1500–1700—Biography—Juvenile literature. I. Title.
PR2895.F36 2013
822.3'3—dc23   [B]   2013030176

CCSS: RL.4.1, 2, 3, 4, 5, 6; RL.5.2, 4, 6, 7; RI.5.1, 2, 3, 8

First Edition
9 8 7 6 5 4 3 2 1